ON THE GO MAZES

Becky Radtke

Dover Publications, Inc.
Mineola, New York

Copyright

Copyright © 2005 by Dover Publications, Inc.
All rights reserved.

Bibliographical Note

On the Go Mazes is a new work, first published by
Dover Publications, Inc., in 2005.

International Standard Book Number

ISBN-13: 978-0-486-44103-0
ISBN-10: 0-486-44103-2

Manufactured in the United States by LSC Communications
44103218   2018
www.doverpublications.com

Note

Everyone is on the go in this little book—from blasting off in a rocket, paddling a canoe, and riding a motorcycle, to driving a double-decker bus, hiking on a trail, and many more travel-related activities. You can help them all get to where they need to go by drawing a line from the beginning arrow to the end. Try to complete all of the mazes before checking the Solutions, which begin on page 52. To have even more fun, color in the finished mazes with crayons or colored pencils. Let's go!

Harry Hound has a nice hot pizza to deliver. Show him the way to get to the house at the end of the path.

4

The driver of the moving van needs to reach the boxes. Help him find the way to get there.

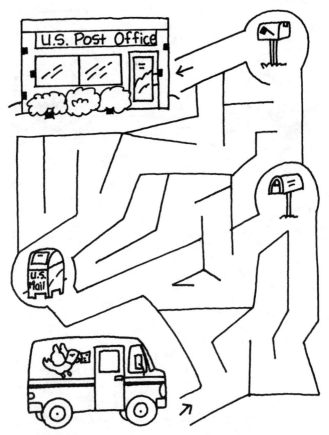

The mail truck must pick up mail on its way to the post office. Find the path that will take it there.

Mama Cat and her kitties need milk fast! Find the path for the milk truck to follow.

This hot air balloon needs to come down to earth safely. Can you find the way?

8

These friends in a dune buggy are ready for some fun at the beach! Please show them the path to take.

9

Show this rocket the way to go to pass four planets and then reach its goal—the Moon!

10

This talented clown is on her way to the circus. Won't you show her the path to take to get to the big tent?

Barney Bear drives a school bus. Find the way for him to go to pick up two students and get to school.

The firefighters just helped put out a blaze. Show
them the path to take to get back to the station.

13

Becky Bunny is riding her new bicycle to the play-
ground. Please help her follow the path.

A special trail leads to the Polar Lodge. Help Bertha Bear find the trail so she can meet her friends at the lodge.

15

Stuart Sheep has been plowing all day. Find the way for him to take to put the tractor back in the barn.

This tourist bus is on its way to the homes of some Hollywood stars. Help it find the way to Fifi, who will sign autographs!

17

Carlos and Timothy need to find their way upstream.
Grab a paddle and show them the way!

18

Show this family in the motor home the path to take to get to the campground. They want to take a dip in the lake.

These hungry workers can't wait for the lunch van to arrive! Show the van driver the way to get to the workers.

Brrr! It's cold! Please help the dog sled find the way to get to the igloo at the end of the path.

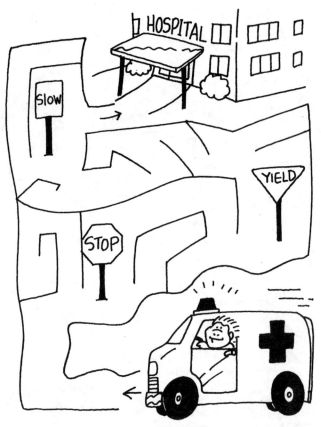

Get out of the way! The ambulance is rushing to the hospital. Find the path to follow to get there.

The Books on the Go bus is coming to town. Help the driver find the way so she can meet the waiting readers.

Lou and Lil plan to have lunch at the picnic table.
Show them the way to get there.

Captain Billy would like to stop at the little island for a rest. Help Billy find the path to get there.

These friends have heard the music from the ice cream truck. Quick! Find the path that will take them to the truck.

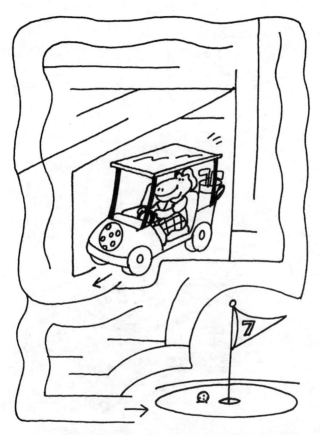

Freddy is on his way to the seventh hole. Show him the way to drive the golf cart to get there.

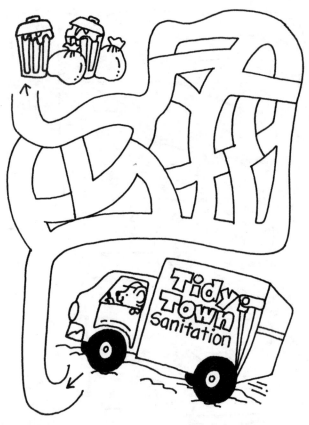

Herman is making his rounds picking up the trash.
Find the path for him to take to the cans and bags.

Patty wants to get to Patrick so that she can get warm by the campfire. Help her find the way.

This ship needs to reach the passengers at the end of the path. Find the way for it to get to them.

These pals are having some winter fun. Show them the way to get to the hot cocoa at the bottom of the hill.

Mike is on his way to help Max move the pile of dirt.
Please help Mike get to Max.

Nellie needs a cab! Show the taxi driver the path to take to get to Nellie.

Candace wants to deliver lumber to a customer. Help her find the way to reach him.

Please guide this jumbo jet down the right path to take it to the airport terminal.

Franny is about to ride her skateboard down the course. Show her the way to get to the ramp at the end.

Penny is in the mood for some tasty fruit. Take her along the path to reach the fruit stand.

This enormous limo is on its way to a party. Won't you show the driver the way to get there?

Sow City is one of the stops for this train. Find the path for the train to take to reach the station.

The race car has almost made it to the finish line.
Show it the way to get there.

This truck must deliver flowers to the birthday girl.
Find the way for it to follow to reach her.

The Dog E. Delivery truck is headed for the office building. Help it find the way there.

A parade just ended on Main Street. Show this street sweeper the way to get there to clean up the mess!

Timmy and Tammy are headed to the top of the mountain. Help them find their way to the end of the trail.

Willie is ready to take a break from driving his truck.
Show him the way to get to the Coffee Cup diner.

The passengers on this double-decker bus can't wait to see the big city. Find the path for them to get there.

The driver of this cherry picker truck needs to get to the orchard. Please show her the way.

Joey is taking his classic car to the car show. He's never been there, so won't you show him the way?

This family has always wanted to see the Cheese Museum! Show them the path to take to get there.

The tanker is on its way to the gas station. Help it find its way through the last few miles.

The soccer game is about to start! Help this minivan find its way to the soccer field.

Solutions

page 4

page 5

page 6

page 7

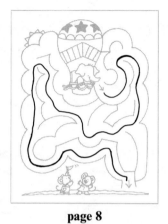

page 8

page 9

page 10

page 11

page 12

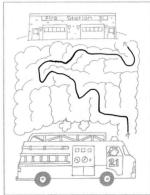

page 13

page 14

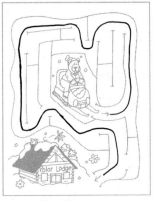

page 15

page 16

page 17

page 18

page 19

page 20

page 21

page 22

page 23

page 24

page 25

page 26

page 27

page 28

page 29

page 30

page 31

page 32

page 33

page 34

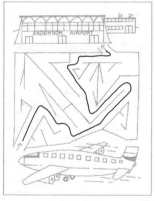

page 35

page 36

page 37

page 38

page 39

page 40

page 41

page 42

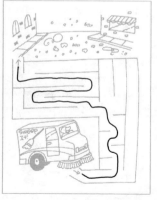

page 43

page 44

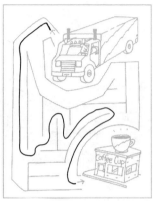

page 45

page 46

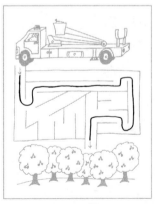

page 47

page 48

page 49

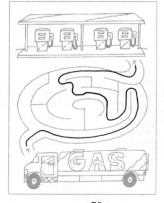

page 50

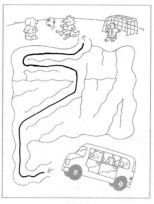

page 51